Rob Hindle

Neurosurgery in Iraq

Templar Poetry

First Published 2008 by Templar Poetry

Fenelon House,
Kingsbridge Terrace
Dale Road, Matlock, Derbyshire
DE4 3NB

www.templarpoetry.co.uk

ISBN 978-1-906285-25-8

A CIP catalogue record for this book is available from the British Library.

For permission to reprint or broadcast these poems write to
Templar Poetry

Typeset by Pliny
Graphics by Paloma Violet
Printed and bound in Turkey

To Lesley

Acknowledgments

Acknowledgements are due to the editors of the following publications in which some of these poems, or versions of them, first appeared: *Dreamcatcher, Staple, The North.* 'Mendigo' was placed third in the Plough Prize 2007 short poem competition. Mark Dunn produced the great drawings for 'Mercenary Man Blues'.

Thanks are due to Jim Caruth and Ann Atkinson for their invaluable criticism and help; to Ray Hearne for support and inspiration in word and deed; and to my family, friends and colleagues for cheering me on. Thanks are also due to Arts Council England (Yorkshire), whose grant gave me time to finish the collection; and to Alex McMillen at Templar Poetry for his wise advice.

ARTS COUNCIL
ENGLAND

Contents

This Vigil

Erebus and Terror

Afrika-Museum, Tervuren

Field Punishment Number One

Blast

This Vigil

'In Spain, the dead are more alive than the dead of any other country in the world.'

- *Lorca*

Valley of the Fallen Dogs

The train stops on a curve
where there is nothing to see
but light, a few still trees
and the splintered remains
of mountains.

Ahead, a tunnel mouth lurks
like a pool. It feels like August,
this waiting, the miles stretching
south into the dust.

This is a frontier, a no-place.
On the map, the signs are all there:
desesperada – hopeless;
aldeaquemada - a village, burnt;

and this *desfiladero*, a gap in the world
where some lost man, dethroned
perhaps and chased from his kingdom,
untied his hounds,
kicked them to the rocks below.

My Father at the May Day Marches

A million people flooding Madrid,
the flags like blossom.

It was a day of all days; you talked
of *La Pasionaria*, how she'd said

it was better to die on your feet
than live on your knees.

Then we walked on,
you silent amid the noise.

Window Cleaner

Carlos is up on the cradle.
He wears a smart red overall,
works quickly and to a high standard.
He is a professional.

The glass is manufactured by Vidur in Barcelona
under the trade mark Climalit.
It is tempered, tinted and double insulating.
It is virtually unbreakable.

Each pane is 220 by 130 centimetres.
If he wished, Carlos could stretch each hand
and touch the top corners while standing
with his feet spread like Leonardo's drawing.

Instead, as he cleans each perfect plane
he watches himself working, the lines
on his neck and brow inked deep
by the refracting properties of the window;

and behind and beyond, still tipped
with ice, the humped tops of the Sierra
de Guadarrama, his childhood home.
As he works, he sings snatches of an old tune.

Mendigo

The beggar

He has taken some trouble.
His hair is oiled and parted,
his empty sleeve pinned
and tucked in a blazer pocket.

Mendigo. It is like a benediction;
but clearly from his level gaze,
from the jut of his chin,

this vigil with its paper cup of coins
is nothing but horror to him.

Dropping a Bottle of Red Wine on the Bank Floor

We are the strangers here,
me sloppy and muttering,
my wife's yellow hair.

Our picnic in a plastic bag
swings mnemonically:
queso manchego, vino tinto.

It is another lovely day,
we agree in English. We smile
so that others can agree.

The guard is bored.
He has nothing to do but look
at us. *¿Americano? ¿Inglés?*

The queue moves and the bag slips:
only the guard doesn't blanch
at the red oozing through the rips.

My Mother with El Greco at the Prado Museum

The saints are craning heavenwards.
They have the ravaged faces of consumptives,
the eyes of maniacs.
Their skin is luminous as bone.

Your hands are long like theirs
but freckled from the sun.
You sway and settle, head still,
a kestrel on a ruffle of air.

The saints have seen something,
a vision, an epiphany.
Your mouth opens slightly
as if to whisper a new word.

At the Seminario

The padre waits to be introduced.
He is used to stillness, the hush
which is his to break. When he speaks
it is like the past, the only recording
of an ancient icon: Caruso; Chopin.
Encantado he chants, welcome
to our home. He turns, then,
shuffles down the hall to his room.

You show us round. The *salón*,
where dust goes up and down
in a pane of sunlight; a kitchen,
sink stacked with cups and smears:
the housekeeper is off
and this is a house of men,
though you're not yet men.

In your study room
are piles of books, a picture
of your mum and dad.
At this distance, Madrid looks foreign
like Manhattan. We stand at the window,
the city miraculous in the heat.
I can't bring you coffee, you say
suddenly. The housekeeper is off.

Eugenie

In memory of Chris Smith, XV International Brigade

Is Eugenie there?
She isn't, just a man
somewhere across the city.

You try again. Eugenie?
No. You pass me the phone,
sit back in your chair.

¿Estas loco? says the voice,
Are you mad?
I apologise, ring off.

It was a long shot,
sixty years, a number
on a scrap of card;

but to you, who carried
this country in your guts
all the long way home,

it was worth the try,
the questioning of your sanity.

Las Gitanas

The gypsy women

At the confusion of the city's edge,
cranes swing slowly over a stream
and a narrow bridge. The building –
glass and steel – seems transitory
and as thin as nylon.

As the bus slows into the turn
we look for the women.
It is harsh as a winter at home
but here, always, we find them
washing clothes on a concrete slab.

Red-armed, laughing, they scrub
bright flowers out of the cold.

In the Wet Towns of Asturias

In October 1934, the miners of Asturias, centred around the town of Mieres, rose in revolt against the Nationalist Government, occupying the city of Oviedo and taking control of much of the area within a few hours. However, Francisco Franco and General Yagüe led Spanish Foreign Legion and government forces to Asturias, landing at Gijón. They brutally put down the uprising in two weeks. The miners had burned churches and killed about 40 people, including 29 priests. The government troops killed an estimated 3,000 and took about 35,000 prisoners, who were tortured and tried well into 1935. The ferocity of the government divided the Spanish people and helped to precipitate the Spanish Civil War of 1936-39.

Mieres

The road has got us nowhere
until on a grinding turn there is nothing
but cloud, filling the valley like a glacier.

In the bus, a stir; newspapers folded,
necks stretched. Somewhere
we have passed into Asturias.

The miners waited in these mountains,
cigar butts clamped in their mouths,
sticks of gelignite held like candles.

We drop into rain, the first houses
blurred and silent. As the road narrows
into a street, the wet stones flash and glimmer.

Blimea

The bar is like a kitchen, yellow lino,
a single, scrubbed table. The woman
pouring cider has the thick red arms
and apron of my mother's aunt.

Outside the day has gone,
the stone roofs along the street
hidden in the wet spring night.
Soon, the clouds will stir, move on

and the moon cut out
the shape of the town: the church,
the *Calle de la Libertad*, the wheels,
jammed and rusting, over the mine.

Gijón

At last, a grey sea.
I'm homesick, imagine
that light blinking from a buoy
might be seen from England
on a clear day.

But here on this low cliff
a stone, raw and brutal as iron.
Before I read the names,
translate the dedication,
I know it is about war.

There is fret in the air,
a salt mist hiding the promontory.
We walk down to the beach,
throw pebbles,
marvel at its stillness.

Erebus and Terror

Perseid Meteor Shower, 1971

There is the sting of frost,
little else. A light comes on
in a neighbour's house;
a door bangs.

In the north sky the milky way
like the shine of the sea.
We wait. I watch how you blow
into your fists. I blow into mine.

The light goes out and in the space
we see a thin white line drop,
a knife's itch drawn on our skin.
Far from the earth, my blooding.

Wincobank

Stand out on the edge,
the river land still and baked
as concrete. Left, a mile off,
cars on the motorway
file through a gap. All day
they are there, wearing, widening.

On the ridge, two teachers
recce a visit. There are nettles,
briars, some glints of bottle.
It's summer at least, the track
from the road just blisters of earth.
There are no nails or needles.

They head back to the car;
the tatters of dandelion clocks
settle in the air. Here, the Brigantes
waited while the legions came:
the flat, ant-ridden stones still
show marks of a fire.

The afternoon goes on. A dog
and a man labour up the bank,
lead limp, redundant. In the valley,
everything the Romans brought
is submersed in silt. On the ridge,
still, the older world juts out.

Veterano

She drinks sweet Spanish brandy and her son says
mum you shouldn't drink on your own and anyway
why Spanish brandy, she says I don't like the French.

She drinks the brandy on her own or sometimes
with Mary from next door; they sit in the kitchen
with the windows open and the sun on the garden.

Later they are quiet and the sun through the brandy
makes her think of the word liquor and the small square
photographs of Fred in Normandy, Dad at the Somme.

Easter Camp

Snow at Easter, my father's plans
cast down by a shift in the wind
and the sullenness of his sons.

He made the best of it – described
with his glove the inky summits
of his own (primordial) childhood:

Rushup Edge, Mam Tor, Lose Hill,
Win Hill. He looked at us, at the snow.
Okay. One walk, then we'll go.

We zipped the tent up and went.
Four brothers, so no need to chat
or chaff: just get it over with.

He chose Lose Hill as it was nearest,
would avoid the stop at some trampled
smudge of path, recourse to the map.

And up we went, and up till,
looking back, our tent was a tiny shock
of orange, dropped on the white peak
fields like a match, still lit.

Loopy

Fear was Connell's dog,
a silence somewhere between
the garage and the house,
the endless rope across the yard.

Fear was the stop at the door,
sun pricking my neck,
the shapes in the glass;
it was grandmother's footsteps,
the what big eyes you have.

It is still the silence,
still the wait for the lurch
of that feral thing, the whip
of the rope uncoiling.
Here I am.

Camping Out

You had just shed your babyhood,
come out lean like me, skin blue
as duck's eggs, shoulders like new bat's wings;
then a bug crept in.

At the hospital I propped you up like a guy.
People looked down at you, up at me.
They brought a syringe as thick as your arm,
hooked up a drip, a monitor.

You were small and still, almost invisible.
When you tried to speak, nothing came out
except your breath's smell. They said
it would take some time: our first night's camping.

You slept, grew slowly back into your self;
l lay listening to the murmur of parents
in a hospital full of children. Outside,
the city grew quiet, the streets empty.

I thought of stars, their light rushing
towards me.

Me and my Daughter Nine Days Old

You will stand one day at the sea's edge,
sinking your skinny feet – you'll have my feet –
into the stinging North Sea silt and laughing.

You will make fairy cakes with me,
breaking egg shells into the fat and sugar,
waiting with a spoon to scour the bowl clean.

One day, you will leave, possibly
trading a hug for the twenty you'll know
is clasped in the fist of your old man.

But today you are nine days old,
it is dawn, and as you sleep I'm slumped
at the table, the tea stewed and forgotten.

Clown

There is still ice
along the bottom road,
still fog by the woods
and the fishing pond.

The frost on the path
near the empty shops
has been there all day:
a crust, treacherous
and grey.

I ginger the car
round the bottom bend
expecting the sudden slip,
the loss of friction.

Then another car
creeping over the hill,
orange wig, white face,
red painted grin strained
and humourless. We pass –

the clown's crossed eyes
fixed straight ahead,
nose thrown onto the passenger shelf
like something bloodied.

Caterwaul

Just a stop on the moor,
two rooms of a farm put up
as a parlour and a public bar.

A woman is feeding sticks
and coals to a smoky fire.
There seem to be dogs everywhere.

The landlord pulls our beer.
His face is long and hollow,
his hair short and thick as foxes' fur.

In a case on the bar
is a cat the size of a weasel.
There is a dark wooden plate.

This cat, it reads, was found
in the wall when the farm was rebuilt.
It was thought to bring luck

to those that lived here.
We take our pints to the window.
Nothing on the road,

on the moor. Behind us
the landlord swears
at the paper he's reading,

the fucking gun law.
The cat looks scared to death,
its pretend eyes flaring as the fire catches.

Cropping Potatoes

10 September 2001

At the end we are on our knees,
scratching the deep ones up
with aching fingers. Then it's done:
the last of this year's crop
laid out on the trodden ground.
We straighten up and drink.
Out west, the moor is comatose:
a stone, a thick flat line, a stone.

We rub off the clay in a plastic bath,
check the ochre skins for worms and rot.
The bad ones make a smallish pile –
a short barrow for a burial.
It feels for a second like a tragedy
but, looking west, I see the same old sky,
the roads and walls, the dark peat
dotted with rocks, and nothing more.

Trailer

Backing his trailer into the allotments
the farmer has caught a metal post,
crooking it like a dandelion stalk.

The post is buried in concrete
under a close-cropped privet hedge.
'I bet they won't be pleased', he says.

He unhooks the trailer and the electrics,
clambers back in and moves up the lane
and back, and up again, nudging

and pulling the post back into position.
We stand by the trailer,
stilled to gawping at the farmer's grace.

Farm

And here is the farmer
in his empty barn, his livestock
and all the subsidies gone

(his wife would go too
if she knew quite how
or had somewhere to go).

And here is the policeman
in the empty lane. He knocks,
but there's no-one.

He knocks again.
And here is the farmer
in his empty barn, his livestock

and all the subsidies gone,
with a picnic of scotch
and his wife's temazepam.

From the Train

From the train a farm, a wall,
a lane of hawthorn. In a month
it will look like a wedding, petal-strewn,
waving. Now it waits out the cold,
the moaning end of winter.

The train cuts north, the soaked fields
full of stones. In the swale of a hill
a scarecrow, dishevelled and forlorn,
gapes stupidly at all the mud.
There are no birds, not one.

Rain comes off the moors, darkness
making mirrors of the windows.
Brake oil warms, sour as formaldehyde,
and we stop. People look around,
the carriage like an unmade bed.

There are sounds: a slam, the frantic
whine of the engine. A local service
whisks by on the other line.
I step into the corridor, stick my face
through the window, the freezing air.

A bag is thrown from the next door
down; a man drops to the gravel,
gathers and bounds out into the fields.
He is tall and bearded, as young as he likes:
Guevara in Cuba or a sixties Christ.

Erebus and Terror

The two ships of Sir John Franklin's 1845 expedition to find the North-west Passage

All this white, pocked on the map
like crazed china. Here was our route
into Wellington Sound and here
the place where the ice sealed us in
through the whole of the winter.

In the straits we'd seen whales
and beneath them in the clear water,
floes, white as bones, like the whales'
huge shadows. The sky had been
littered with upturned cliffs.

At Devon Island were the strange
remains of a camp: six hundred
food cans piled in a mound, some still
unopened. Across a small channel
were signs of a burial.

We laboured round, looking back
at the ice seized ship. By the cairn
there were traces of a fire,
some sledge tracks leading away
inland. We unearthed the bones

and overcoats of three men.
The captain said The Lord's Prayer
and we covered them again.
Of the Erebus and the Terror
we found not a thing.

Etna

There are chickens on this train
and the woman who is holding them
like loaves under each arm
has eyes like chickens, brows
brown and rutted as a cart track.

Circumetnea, something mythic,
a train line coiled round ancient Etna.
But this clatter, this waft of drains,
this old man with his paper
could be Rome, Milan, Manchester.

Gradually we climb away from the sea.
Every station is smoke and chatter,
each neighbour hailed like he's home
from war, not the next village
or bar or the market in Catania.

At Randazzo there seems nothing
but heat. Even seconds on the open
platform is enough to madden us,
send us reeling for the wrong way out.
The chicken woman scuttles up the street,

her charges slumped, half ready
for the pot. All the fires and spit
of the mountain have never touched
this place, the closest to the summit.
Empty now, it seems dead in any case:

in the piazza, rows of plastic seats
and amps rigged up on a metal frame;
shop doors and windows shuttered;
and at the end of town, a low wall
below the moon-dry mountain.

Low Season

A whale, hump-backed, juvenile,
rolled dead up the beach at Runswick
and stopped, the first October tide's
collateral. Around it yards of wrack
and kelp, one tatty wing of a gull.

It measured almost thirty feet
and was the colour of Welsh slate.
Along its belly and flukes, white
marks like barnacle beds. There it lay
in the sand like a shelf of stone.

A woman, traipsing the sea edge
back along the bay, came on it
suddenly in the grainy evening,
its mussel-bed smell, one plane-prop fin,
an eye just holding the black horizon.

By the time they took it away
(three sections lumped somehow
into a truck) it stank. The humpback,
famous for its song, shutting windows
and disturbing everyone.

Connemara

A flickering coast appears at every turn
then swings away as a creeping inlet
bends the road northwards.
Mist rests over crumpled fields
and stones and sheep are strewn like shattered teeth.
At a bridge the bog has leached through the wall.

This is a conquered place. A fellow
on the road at Cashel trips his stick
in lieu of a trotting horse like a blind man
heading for home who, for all his certainty,
smells nothing in the world but storms.

Yet when he turns and holds his hand
at his brow, his eye is clear blue;
and the blue of his eye has the sea
in it and the fleeting Connemara sky;
and his hair, blue-black like the shapes
of birds thrown up against the gold of Inish Maan,
shines like a song in the coming rain.

Afrika-Museum, Tervuren

The Africa-Museum at Tervuren in Belgium opened in 1897 as the Royal Museum for Central Africa. It has the most extensive collection of Central African ethnographic objects in the world, including the entire archives of Henry Morton Stanley.

Zoomorphic Loi slit drum

A single trunk
carved thin and thick,
a two-tone telegraph
for the *Bantu*.

It is shaped like the antelope
who is quick
and hears everything.
It is hollow.

Listen at the slit:
someone is coming
says the drum;
we must go.

Yombe pot lid

When she brings my food
the pot is covered with a lid,
a gift from her mother.

It is carved into a proverb:
three men, a turtle, a sleeping woman,
a gun laid on the ground.

When she brings my food
in a covered pot, I know
there is something on her mind;

but the men are silent
and I cannot wake the woman
and the turtle is inscrutable

inside his shell.
There is only a gun, then
and a food pot cover.

Samsa 'thumb piano'

Play us your life,
your days by the forest,
the sounds of your night.

Show us your hands,
your palms and fingers
raised at the light.

See? That is heaven
where the father lives.
Now, open your eyes.
Forgive us.

Nkisi Nkonde nail fetish figure

The children have seen the giraffe
and the crocodile. They've wrecked
the café. One was told off saying
'wank' in the reptile gallery.
There is only the shop and the toilets
and they'll be on their way.

The last boy wanders through the wrong room
where there is a bundled figure of cloth,
or bark, with a wooden face.
Its mouth is open as if singing;
its eyes are closed. It has a magic box
on its head, another at its stomach.
There are nails stuck in it. They look cold.

The boy remembers he needs the loo
and goes. On the coach and later,
on the boat, he worries about the nails.
The bundled figure listens: he was sure
his people had come back to wake him.

Tabwa buffalo mask

You would dance
to welcome a birth

You would dance
to celebrate the harvest

You would dance
when death came, or sickness

You would dance
to tell the great stories

When you danced
the people danced

When you danced
the spirits of the old ones danced

When you danced
the gods would wake up and listen

When you danced
the people would know what to do

You would dance
before a great battle

Now there are no people
the spirits are lost
the gods sleep on

and when you move
it is just the breeze coming through the door
or cold hands flicking at the dust

45

Bula Matari

When you found Livingstone
you thought you'd made it,
pictured the crowds on the Mall,
the flags, the Queen;

but as you sat with him
by the lakeshore, saw how he looked
at you, so still, eyes burning
with the green of the jungle,

then you knew what he was
and how a piecer from the Lanark mills
could make a life to live in;
and you cursed yourself

who could never be like him.
They called you Bula Matari,
Breaker of Rocks; but look,
you say, at what I gave them:

roads to the coast; hard steel;
the word of the one true God.
Did I not deliver them:
bring Africa to the world?

Scud

15 January 1991. US forces launch an air assault against targets in Iraq.

When the world ends, it will be
a Sunday night in January

like every Sunday night you had
as a child. You will fill it with strange

sounds – the whine of an engine
on the next hill, the creep

and murmur of something elemental.
There will be the bass notes

of voices from the floor below
from which you get only the tone:

query, insistence, uncertainty.
Outside, the three-legged cat

from across the road will arch
and spit at its spiky shadow;

the dog that barks and barks all day
will twitch and worry at a dream.

And somewhere, like this Sunday
night, some men will walk out

of a meeting room and down a hall,
falling in step as they have always done.

They'll walk to the end, to a room
back-lit with banks of lurid screens.

And like tonight a clock will come
to nothing and everywhere

soft points of light will flicker on.

Field Punishment Number One

Mercenary Man Blues

I remember in seventh grade, we read this poem

by Robert Frost about taking the road less traveled

and I guess that's what I done

I reckon

Cultural Orientation: An Introduction for Marines

Sandals are the norm
They will be strewn about the door to the home

Men wear long button-up robes called dishdashas
which we call man-dresses
This is also normal

Sleeping may occur in almost any room
There are no beds and everyone huddles together on the floor
There is no equivalent to pajamas

Everyone smokes, though women do it generally in the house

Everyone drinks tea, which is strong and served with great ceremony

It is common to see two people of the same gender holding hands
whether it is two women or two men
This is normal

Baghdad Dentist

'...one of the national guards came asking for removal of calculus around his teeth, it's a cleaning of teeth with an ultrasound device. He was listening to the loud music of his mobile and sat on the dental chair with a gun in his hand...'

- posted at 7.41pm, 15 February 2008 on the Baghdadentist blog

Your eyes open wide
as I start the drill,
pull the lamp in closer.

Between us, your gun
and your clenched hands;
your life and mine.

I turn on the pump,
peer in. An ordinary mouth:
teeth broken, teeth missing.

I work quickly,
try to breathe slowly.
Through my glove I can feel

the drill's detonations,
feel you tighten and relax
and tighten. We both

expect pain and fear it.
Soldier and dentist,
in this city the same.

Cert PG

'Moderate violence, without detail, may be allowed if justified by its setting.'
-British Board of Film Classification

So we're downtown on Haifa Street and it's   uh
quiet   we're all good   everybody's good   I'm
with Vasquéz Cabrera and Cato and Cato's   uh
he's lookin pretty freaked but we're okay   we're
good   Then BLAM an ied hits the Stryker in
front and Cato starts shoutin and shootin
everywhere but he's hittin shit Then they're all
frikkin over us and Cato and Cabrera are both
shoutin and givin it out at at at at at at at   and
Vasquéz   he's drivin   he's goin Jesus Christ
we're gettin the fuck outa here and we're past
the Stryker which is stuck with no power still the
motherfuckers everywhere   Then a car comes
across us and Vasquéz hits it hard and it spins
and stops and we're outa there with Cato and
Cabrera givin some to the people in the car
which I think   uh   well they might have been
women I saw   two women and two kids who
just got caught up in the crossfire

In Karbala

'2 million people squeezed into this one place and not even a small fight...'
- posted by Salam, 1.00am, 3 March 2004 on the Where is Raed? blog

Raed sends a message to himself.
It is five days until Ashura,
the holy day of al-Hussein:
you should get your ass in Karbala.

He will grow a beard, he says,
go there with his mother and his cousin.
They will adhere to the holy rituals
and wear black and remember.

I frikkin' met an Ayatollah!
I watched him eating, then
he came and put his hands on my face,
blessed me, blessed my mother.

Then there were mortars falling
and everything was noise and ruin.
Thank God we were out of the centre
where the shrines and the bombs were.

All that horror, but four hours later
it was just as before.
That was what happened in Karbala:
one amazing thing after another.

Found poem: Red2Alpha's Post

posted at 4.40am, 30 May 2007 on the This is Your War II blog

The last time you see him
is in a black bodybag
intabation tube in his mouth
eyes glassed over
skin waxy, like a dead fish
in the market.

Neurosurgery in Iraq

'All patients with Parkinsonism and movement disorders can be treated now in Iraq by Deep Brain Stimulation (DBS)... All Iraqi patients can be referred now to the Neurosciences Hospital in Baghdad on Monday to be seen in the movement disorders clinic.'

- posted by Dr Haitham H Shareef, 5.11am, 18 March 2008 on the
Neurosurgery in Iraq blog

Last Monday
was a bomb in the market

My sister was buying shoes there
only an hour before

I felt the explosion,
heard pieces of concrete
smashing in the yard

Wednesday was the visit
to the surgery

There was a checkpoint
on Damascus Street
so we were late

Dr Hanif had good news
about a clinic at the hospital

He wrote a letter
and gave it to my sister
said we must go there on Monday

but that is not a good day
to go anywhere

Blast

'These boys with old, scared faces, learning to walk.'
- Siegfried Sassoon, 'Survivors'

1

This soldier caught an improvised bomb.
His skull was fractured, eardrum blown out,
left eye injured. Part of his brain suffered
severe contusion. Unconscious for ten days,
they took out a chunk of his skull so his brain
could swell. Then they flew him home.

He had forgotten the names of things,
had to relabel them with word games.
He remembered seeing tubes with metal wings
flying into two towers; remembered
the city of dust lit up with orange clouds,
people lying on roads in pools of red.

Now he stays home with his wife, this woman
who laughs at his jokes again and again.
He went to the game one time: the Nationals
hit a home run and everyone cheered, and he cheered
with them; thing was, he could hear himself
cheering. So he prefers to stay home.

2

This soldier, we will call him x,
has suffered a full blast injury.
Both eyes have been lost as you can see;
There is a subdural hemotoma here,
and bruising to the brain tissue here.
The left forearm was severely damaged
with compound fractures here and there.
We have done some remodelling
of the hand. He lost the index finger,
so we relocated the middle digit
and released the tendons to give him a grip.
We're quite pleased with that.

In terms of rehab, he has OT to work on
visualization and manual dexterity.
He suffered some traumatic brain injury
resulting in migraines, memory loss,
depression and anxiety: the usual things.
He's soon to be transferred to a new programme
of intensive blind-rehabilitation in Chicago.
Then let's watch him go, hey soldier?

3

there was a programme on the History Channel last night
it was about Shell Shock in WWI
they thought it was cowardice these men shaking and shouting
and shitting their pants (I mean literally folks!)
so they had something called Field Punishment Number One
where they tied you to a fixed object like a post
or even a crucifix made of trench boards
and then every day your platoon would carry you out
within range of enemy shells and leave you there
two hours each day for maybe two or three months
Fuck! If you were bad before sure to god you'd be crazy after!
I have to say the History Channel makes you think
makes me think for sure